UNDERSTANDING
THE
TIMES

JAN MARKELL

HARVEST PROPHECY
AN IMPRINT OF HARVEST HOUSE PUBLISHERS

All Scripture quotations are taken from the (NASB®) New American Standard Bible®, Copyright © 1960, 1971, 1977, 1995, 2020 by The Lockman Foundation. Used with permission. All rights reserved. www.lockman.org.

Cover design by Studio Gearbox

Cover images © Dima Zel, d1sk / Shutterstock

Interior design by KUHN Design Group

For bulk, special sales, or ministry purchases, please call 1-800-547-8979.
Email: CustomerService@hhpbooks.com

Understanding the Times
Copyright © 2025 by Jan Markell
Published by Harvest House Publishers
Eugene, Oregon 97408
www.harvesthousepublishers.com

ISBN 978-0-7369-8962-6 (pbk)
ISBN 978-0-7369-8963-3 (eBook)

Library of Congress Control Number: 2024935689

Printed in the United States of America

24 25 26 27 28 29 30 31 32 33 / BP / 10 9 8 7 6 5 4 3 2 1

This book is dedicated to all those who long for truth and who wish to understand the times, contend for the faith, and be watchmen on the wall in this chaotic generation. We live in a time like no other that is distorted by fake news, deception, delusion, and false teaching. All those who strive to see beyond this fog are a great encouragement to me.

This book is also dedicated to those who long for our Lord's appearing.

We will soon enjoy our crown.

2 TIMOTHY 4:8

CONTENTS

CHAPTER 1

A FRONT-ROW SEAT TO THE LAST ACT

have considered myself a watchman on the wall for many years. There is never a shortage of news or events to highlight as our planet groans with wars and rumors of wars, moral and spiritual decline, and rampant apostasy.

Even so, God is doing good things too! Not everything reported today deals with how the sky is falling. God is saving souls, and Bible prophecies are being fulfilled. So much is happening that it is a challenge to keep up with it all. So when it comes to world events and Bible prophecy, commentators, columnists, authors, and pundits have to be selective. That is not easy.

Our Times—Not a Pretty Picture!

First Chronicles 12:32 says that the sons of Issachar were men who understood the times. That suggests that God's people need to understand what on earth is happening. And the only way to do that is to understand what the Bible says about our times.

Here are some thoughts for starters.

Second Timothy 3:1-7 is a powerful passage that talks about the character of fallen mankind during the last days. It's not a pretty picture! *Perilous times will come.* People will be self-focused. They will be covetous, boastful, proud, blasphemous, unthankful, unholy, and without natural affection. There will be little respect for parents. And people will be marked by a "form of godliness" (verse 5)—they might look good on the outside, but it's a completely different story on the inside.

People will be lovers of pleasure more than lovers of God. *If it feels good, do it!* They will call evil good, and call good evil (Isaiah 5:20). People will be so bad because of reprobate thinking that God will give "them over to a debased mind, to do those things which are not fitting, being filled with all unrighteousness" (Romans 1:28-29).

People will also gravitate toward false theology (1 Timothy 4:1). This means solid churches will be hard to find. There will be many wolves among the flock (Acts 20:29).

Most troubling of all, "the spirit of the antichrist" (1 John 4:3) is already here, even before the Antichrist—whom I call Mr. Fix-It—will turn up on the world scene during the end times. By then, believers will have already been raptured from the earth. But his influence precedes him, even before his appearance.

A Front-Row Seat for the Last Act

Our world is getting worse. At first we might think, *Who would want to be an end-times Christian?* However, we have been called for such a time as this, and we are here on assignment! It is a privilege and a challenge to be alive in these days. *We have a front-row seat to the last act.* The drama has become intense. The players are all in place. The stage is being set. And you can't understand the times without developing a biblical perspective that helps to shine the light of God's truth on everything.

When it comes to understanding the times, our school education doesn't matter. If we don't know what the Bible says about life during the last days, we'll be vulnerable to deception. If we don't know God's prophetic word, we will be lost in a sea of terrifying headlines that make no sense.

The way our world is coming apart at the seams, our human inclination will be to hide in a storm shelter until things get better. But that's not what God desires of us as Christians. And sadly, too many churches are leaving their flocks unprepared for these last days.

Game Changers

From a prophetic standpoint, there have been many game changers all through the history of mankind. And lately, they've become more frequent. When I began a radio outreach in the spring of 2001, I had no idea how much the world would change in the days to come.

One example is what took place on September 11, 2001. I simply was not prepared. Sure, I had been to Israel, and I had seen the Arab-Israeli conflict firsthand during the 1980s. I knew that Islam would be a major end-times player, but not to the degree that it has played out since that fateful day.

Now I am watching so much more—new wars, pandemics, economic turmoil, governments taking greater control and leading us toward globalism, and all sorts of happenings that can be called apocalyptic without being sensational. Today's crises are truly stunning. They are coming fast and furious.

On many days, I feel overwhelmed. And if this longtime watchman is taken aback, I can imagine what others are feeling!

On October 7, 2023, another game-changing event took place. It was a wake-up call for the world, and especially for Jewish people everywhere. Hamas terrorists invaded southern Israel and slaughtered 1,200 innocent Israelis. This horror scene alone would have been sufficiently shocking, but the calamity didn't end there. Much of the world turned their backs on Jewish people and made them the targets of antisemitic attacks. I will address that later in this book.

Following that fateful day, the spread of what I call Israel Derangement Syndrome increased all the more. You would think people would have been sympathetic toward the victims of a terror attack. But not when it comes to Israel. Rioters and protesters in many countries held up signs that read "Long live Hamas!" *The world was cheering for barbarians!*

Who could have imagined that would happen? Jewish society and culture has long been a blessing to the whole world. Yet today, the Jews are being hated and hunted down as they were in Europe in the 1930s and 1940s.

Hadn't a world war put an end to Jew hatred? Hadn't haunting scenes from the Holocaust caused the world to say, "Enough!"— to the point of creating a Jewish national homeland? This was to be a place where Jews could always be safe—a place created in a

United Nations vote that said Jewish torment had to come to an end. There was almost universal agreement about this.

At the time Israel became a nation again, America stepped up to the plate and led the way. President Harry Truman abandoned his advisors, who had urged him to move on and not side with the Jews. But Truman said no. He would be like the ancient King Cyrus, who, many centuries earlier, had allowed the Jewish captives in Babylon to return home.

Hunted Once Again

Out of the slaughter of Jewish innocents in southern Israel came a world on edge. Jews stopped wearing Jewish symbols. In France, radicals spray-painted the Star of David on Jewish homes, targeting them for antisemitic attacks. In other parts of the world, Jews were hunted and threatened. Jewish students at universities hid in dorm rooms or cafeterias while antisemites pounded on doors with the intent to hurt them.

The scenes were shocking and even terrifying. *If you were a Jew, it was clearly 1938 in Germany all over again.* That's the year when a wave of violence against Jews exploded, culminating in Kristallnacht, or the Night of Broken Glass. That's when large mobs all over Germany vandalized and destroyed synagogues, businesses, and homes, and murdered hundreds of Jews. Thousands more were arrested in the weeks afterward.

But after October 7, 2023, the violence against Jews surfaced all over the world—not only in Germany. Hundreds of thousands were enraged by an anti-Jewish bloodlust that terrified even non-Jews. Christians were left in shock. This was clearly a new day. If ever Isaiah 40:1-2 was appropriate, it was now:

> "Comfort, comfort My people," says your God.
> "Speak kindly to Jerusalem."

Look Up and Not Around

In the upcoming chapters, we'll look at the tide of our times from a biblical and prophetic perspective. While we could easily be discouraged by all that's going wrong, I want to remind us we're to live with anticipation in these amazing times—and consider our place in God's end-times plans. We are to be "encouraging one another; and all the more as you see the day drawing near" (Hebrews 10:25).

As fellow watchmen, we can't merely sound a warning. We are to prepare people for what is happening, encourage them to understand the times, and urge them to look up to God and not around at the world.

If God has you here on assignment, then shouldn't you view this as an amazing time to be alive?

CHAPTER 2

TRENDING TOWARD THE TRIBULATION

hear from people all over the world. Many of them ask, "How can we possibly live in such mind-numbing times yet have so many Christians who aren't even asking, 'What does all of this mean?'"

Perhaps you know friends and family members who truly love the Lord yet are indifferent to today's events. And they choose to ignore the one-third of the Bible that deals with prophecy. In many cases, it's because reality has turned too negative for these people.

I'll never forget this e-mail:

> Jan, I am viewed as crazy just because I talk about how excited I am for the Lord to return, or about the times we live in. I've become downright nervous about even mentioning world news and events, or end-times prophecies. The reaction from fellow believers is volatile. I am having trouble finding *even*

one person in my life who would be willing to discuss any of today's issues. What is most disheartening is the indifference of my church of 30 years (emphasis added).

Weary Watchmen, Alone and Isolated

Chaos and evil have accelerated, as the Bible said would happen. But interest in learning about the end times is surprisingly low. And too many weary watchmen are alone and isolated. Most of the people they mingle with are waiting for normal to return and for life to carry on. Some are waiting for a forthcoming election that they believe will put society back on the right track. There is always some earthly hope that people are holding out for.

But the Bible says that humanity will get worse. The world is being prepped for the Antichrist. Though prophecy-loving believers try to warn others, their words are falling on many deaf ears. Christians who proclaim caution about the rough road ahead are being marginalized—they are being pushed to the back of the proverbial bus and told to settle down and be quiet.

World leaders have no comprehension that when it comes to fixing problems, they are majoring on the minors. To them, it makes perfect sense to obsess over things like carbon emissions and business regulations. But during the tribulation, issues like this will fade in significance as they cope with seal and trumpet and bowl judgments. God's judgments will spark a vastly different kind of "climate change" they cannot imagine!

Prophecy-informed believers are warning about the days ahead, saying that the whole world is trending toward the tribulation. But too few have ears to hear.

We Cannot Be Silent, or the Blood Is on Our Hands

While it is discouraging that so few people have any interest in understanding the times, we cannot be silent. Ezekiel 33:6 tells us that if we as watchmen don't warn others, their blood is on our hands. So we cannot be silent.

There are terrible consequences when people don't do things God's way. Society will fail. The church will fall away into apostasy. But prideful mankind always thinks his way is best, and wreckage results.

In recent decades, as interest in the rapture has diminished in the church, so has interest in everything else about the end times—Israel's key role in the last days, the trends that indicate we are getting nearer to the tribulation, the building of the third temple in Jerusalem, the increase of end-times deception, the rush toward a cashless society and central bank digital currency, and so much more!

Because much of the church has become silent on these issues, it has become more difficult for people to find help when they want to understand the times. There are many who are asking earnest questions as they observe the turmoil of our day. If the pulpits and Sunday school classes are not addressing our times, people will buy the lies offered by the secular world and media. Or the lies of skeptics. Or the dismissal of friends and family who think all talk about the end times is silly.

So, we cannot be silent.

Occupy Until He Comes

Though we know we are trending toward the tribulation, that does not mean we should be nervous or scared. As watchmen during these last days, we are called to be *watching and waiting*. We are to *occupy* until He comes. We're to *look up*.

The good news for us as believers is we will not experience the tribulation—also known as the time of Jacob's trouble, or Daniel's seventieth week. We have no reason for fear and dread. In fact, we should be excited! The prophets of old longed to be a part of our generation. Today, Bible prophecy is unfolding before our eyes, and God has us here for His reasons. We are here on assignment!

The Lord God of the universe has entrusted us for such a time as this. Don't grow weary in whatever assignment He has for you!

CHAPTER 3

THE GREAT RESET: HIDING IN PLAIN SIGHT

For some time now, a scheme has been unfolding with the help of a group of global elites. A key part of it involves dismantling capitalism and installing global socialism and Marxism. They are calling for governments all over the world to cooperate with one another. They believe a global model of governance is needed, which ultimately, will lead to tyrannical rule and will pave the way to usher in the Antichrist.

I am not sure these global movers and shakers realize this. But we do know that they will eagerly embrace this "man with a plan" when he arrives on the world scene.

I hope that has your attention. I'm not writing this to be sensational, but rather, to inform you of what is happening.

The world's globalists, led by founder Klaus Schwab and his World Economic Forum (WEF), have waited a long time.

They have been moving in the shadows—and out in the open—preparing the way for what will inevitably lead to a one-world system of government. While there have been other efforts in the past by those who have wanted global dominion, this current effort has been rallying around certain problems and issues over the past several decades, and proposing ways to fix them.

Then when COVID came along, Schwab and his fellow elites at the World Economic Forum called for The Great Reset.

Remaking the World

The intent of The Great Reset is to remake the world according to the vision held by Schwab and those of like mind with him. Their ideas are all laid out on the WEF website. A few years ago, on both its website and Facebook page, the WEF presented eight predictions for the future.[1] One of them is "You'll own nothing, and you'll be happy." To do this is to abolish private property—a thoroughly Marxist concept.

The WEF also says we need a new and sustainable model for urban development, what they call 15-minute cities.[2] Everything you need will be a convenient and short walking distance from you. But all of this will come at great costs to your personal freedoms. Central to this idea is the banning of car ownership. According to *The Wall Street Journal*, "If the World Economic Forum (WEF) has its way, the number of cars around the world will be reduced by 75% by 2050."[3]

The WEF is trying to convince the world how wonderful it will be when we own nothing and are happy. But Marxist systems of government have never worked—and they have surely made no one happy! In fact, in countries under Communist rule over the past 100 years, it is estimated that as many as 100 million people have been killed or died from unnatural deaths.[4]

We are moving in the direction where "contrary content" in speech or print will not be permitted. Certain products will be allowed, and others will not. Fossil fuels will be replaced by green technologies. Societies will become cashless, and all monetary transactions will be replaced by digital currency controlled by government-run banks. This means a person's ability to use their own money could be canceled by governing authorities at the slightest provocation.

Under global authorities who will make all decisions about how businesses, healthcare organizations, education institutions, and more are to be managed, the middle class and small entrepreneurs will be wiped out. All this will be done in the name of making everyone equal and making them secure from the ravages of competition, risk, and chance.

And the Christian faith will be suppressed.

The global elites at the WEF boast about their goals, but their aspirations go against the natural human inclinations for autonomy and freedom. Yet these globalists will persuade people, saying that it's necessary for us as individuals to make sacrifices for the greater good of all. In this way, they will convince people to go along with this new system. Globalists believe their ideas will lead to a paradise that will solve the world's problems. But that's because they will be the few who are in control.

Pandemic Panic

Up till now, the most effective enabler of The Great Reset was the COVID pandemic unleashed in late 2019 and early 2020. The resulting panic took the planet by storm, filled entire populations with abject fear, and led to massive lockdowns. Government mandates were forced upon America and other nations.

A cabal of tyrants told us we had to shut down, wear masks, and no longer associate with one another in close proximity. Some restrictions were imposed by threat of incarceration and fines.

In a relatively short span of time, societies around the world were transformed beyond recognition. Constitutional rights were suspended. Dissent was censored. Government officials issued edicts restricting the most basic aspects of our lives—where we could go, when we could go there, how long we were allowed to spend there, how many friends we were allowed to meet there. We were managed almost like inmates in a prison. Many livelihoods were intentionally ruined as the global population was bullied and humiliated so that they would be "compliant."

What we cryptically call "the left" is, of course, *always* trying to reset, reform, or transform the world, as the left holds to a fundamentally revolutionary worldview.

This Is Nothing but the New World Order

For years, American politicians have demanded that we transform America. They may try to soften the blow by suggesting it is time to "change America." But as some have rightfully pointed out, there are many who do not want to change the qualities they love about America. It is only those who wish to tear down

American ways and values who have this mindset. Freedom-loving people simply want to hang on to the wonderful liberties that our Founding Fathers established.

But the world's globalists are against any kind of national individualism that makes it more difficult for them to achieve their goals. This includes the schemers at the World Economic Forum, the United Nations, the World Bank, the International Monetary Fund, the World Trade Organization, and other globalist-minded organizations.

The elites who continue to promote The Great Reset are using it as a mask to usher in the new world order. In the meantime, our world hangs on the precipice of eternity as signs of the rapidly approaching tribulation gain in intensity and frequency each day.

How much of this hideous system will believers see? Will some of it be installed before we are raptured prior to the tribulation? For Christians, isn't the *real* reset the arrival of the millennium and the new heavens and the new Earth? While we don't know how far along The Great Reset will be when God raptures us, for sure we are now seeing the setup for this future global tyrannical system.

The Great Reset Has a Great Problem: The Church

The satanic plan is making progress, and it will eventually lead to the rise of the Antichrist—but not as long as those who constitute the church of Jesus Christ are still a part of this world. While we may be watching the setup, the Bible guarantees we are not appointed to remain on Earth once the Antichrist is revealed. We are not destined for God's wrath (1 Thessalonians 5:9).

Make no mistake—globalism fits into the apocalyptic scheme for the last days, but it won't catch God by surprise. He has known about what will happen since before the beginning of time. And as long as the church remains on this earth, The Great Reset has a great problem.

Once the church is removed in the rapture, all hell will break loose. Those who want their Great Reset will get their wishes, but it won't be a picnic. Quite the opposite. Instead, they will find themselves in the coming tribulation, during which God will judge a godless mankind.

God Sits in the Heavens and Laughs!

Mankind's scheme will go up in smoke. Humanity will try its best but will fail. Those who are evil cannot succeed at anything but for a short season. The movers and shakers of the future world system will turn to one another for help as their empires come crumbling down around them. They will think their wisdom and power made them unstoppable. And they will be wrong.

God will sit in the heavens and laugh at them (Psalm 2:4). He will rebuke them in His anger. He will reduce their empires to ashes. And He will assign them to a godless eternity.

After destroying mankind's final empire, God will install His Son Jesus as king in Zion—in Jerusalem—and we will rule with Him during His thousand-year reign!

This is the believer's glorious reset. And I hope you are looking forward to it.

CHAPTER 4

WHAT HAPPENED
TO MY CHURCH?

Y̶ou would be amazed at the huge volume of emails Olive Tree
Ministries receives about troubling church issues and about
the perils of those who are trying to find a good church—especially
one that is willing to teach Bible prophecy. Tragically, there are
many pastors and churches that are silent about prophecy, the
end times, and Israel's place in God's plans for the future. When
the Christians who are part of these congregations ask about this
silence, they are often rebuked or criticized. These emails would
fill a book, which would be a page-turner!

There are many Christians who, up until October 7, 2023,
didn't notice that their church never talked about prophecy and
Israel. For whatever reason, they simply didn't realize they weren't
being taught about these important topics.

Why on October 7, 2023? That's when Israel got an unex-
pected wake-up call from terrorists in Gaza. On that day, the

world was forever changed. Demon-inspired fighters for Hamas were unleashed on Israel—fighters who were dedicated to annihilating the Jews. More than 1,200 innocent Israelis were killed that day. And nearly 250 more were kidnapped by the brutal barbarians who had invaded southern Israel.

A Rude Awakening

In the weeks that followed, church members around the world had a rude awakening as well. They were stunned about their church's silence about the attack. Some of these people had attended their church for years or even decades. They loved their church family and felt the pulpit was sound, even if their pastors or teachers neglected some topics that were near and dear to their hearts.

It so happens that Israel is near and dear to many Christians. When the Jewish nation was brutally attacked, many believers assumed that their church would stand with Israel that following Sunday. They were sure that their church would be front and center by way of prayer, support, and even financial aid.

Yet large numbers of Christians were shocked. Not only was their church silent that next Sunday, but for weeks and months to come. Heart-to-heart conversations with pastors and church leaders produced little fruit. For a variety of reasons, there are churches and leaders who simply don't want to talk about what had happened in Israel and why it is biblically significant.

Clearly, something was wrong. How could this be?

War Isn't Seeker Sensitive

A few decades ago, the seeker-sensitive movement swept through the church. One of the key goals of this movement was to attract people to church by making it a feel-good experience for both believers and unbelievers. Difficult topics and issues were avoided, and the constant emphasis was on positivity and building people's self-esteem.

While the seeker-sensitive movement itself has since diminished, its effects are still widely felt. Whether intentionally or not, many churches today want to focus only on the positive and are reluctant to address negative issues.

It is true that the headlines, photos, and videos that came out of southern Israel in October 2023 were horrific and grim. They would not make for a feel-good experience. Talking about the conflicts between Israel and her terrorist neighbors would not fit into any church-growth strategy. Many church leaders fear that talking about the Middle East will create division in their congregations. Much of this fear comes from lacking a clear understanding of Bible prophecy and of the issues at stake in the Middle East.

Evil rose to a new level on October 7, 2023, and in fact, spread far beyond the Mideast. Antisemitism has exploded in countries everywhere. Some people have even wondered if all of this could escalate and eventually lead us to World War III. That's how much the conflict between Israel and her terrorist neighbors has changed the landscape internationally.

Perhaps your church was among those that didn't want to make people feel uncomfortable. But isn't prayer one of the greatest weapons we have for fighting against evil? And that would include prayer for the peace of Jerusalem! (Psalm 122:6).

The Silence of the Shepherds Is Rooted in Wrong Theology

Ever since October 7, 2023, I have heard many times every day about the silence of the shepherds when it comes to what's happening in Israel. Some people have asked: Could this silence be rooted in a church's theology? The answer is a resounding yes!

I encourage all believers to do a study on biblical theology. And because prophecy and Israel are both such major topics in the Bible, it's vital for us to understand what Scripture teaches about them.

There are certain kinds of theology that affect a pastor's or church's views on prophecy and Israel. These include replacement theology, covenant theology, amillennialism, Dominion theology, preterism, and more. You may find that you are not in agreement with what these views teach about prophecy and Israel, and yet your church may be promoting them.

To be blunt, this explains why many churches today are silent about Israel. Their theology doesn't fit with what we see in the news headlines. When Israel was invaded on October 7, 2023, many churches ignored what had happened because it was inconvenient for them. Because they teach that Israel has been replaced by the church—as taught in replacement theology, or supercessionism—they say Israel no longer has a unique place in God's plan. So they conclude there is no reason to pay attention to Israel.

Some Christians think theology is boring or complicated. *But it is important!* Very simply, biblical theology is the study of God and the Christian faith, and what we believe will affect how we live. My purpose in this book isn't to define and explore theology, but most of the above-mentioned theologies teach *that God has cast away His people Israel due to their rejection of Christ and unbelief.* Many major denominations embrace this way of thinking. And it is why they have been silent.

But what happened on October 7, 2023, was the essence of evil. Not only that, it is part of the stage-setting that God is doing for the end times and Christ's return. These are good reasons for pastors and churches to talk about what is taking place. Pastors especially should lead their congregations in the battle against evil!

People are now tired of the silence of the shepherds. Our world is too volatile, too angry, and too evil for us to stand on the sidelines and be silent. We must take a stand and make sure we have a correct understanding of what the Bible says about Israel.

The Eleventh Commandment: Thou Shalt Not Offend

Theology is one reason many shepherds have been silent about Israel and Bible prophecy. Another reason is what we could call the "eleventh commandment": *Thou shalt not offend.* Taking a stand on potentially divisive issues is discouraged. We're told not to talk about current events. Church leaders have become afraid to shine biblical light on matters that relate to politics and voting. And they fear that talking about the prophetic signs of the times will only scare people.

Many churches today prefer to focus on love, unity, and

tolerance. We're told we must be known for what we agree on, not what we disagree on. Everything and everyone must be accepted, and we shouldn't speak out against sin. For these reasons, more and more churches have become places where people "will not endure sound doctrine," and instead, "they have itching ears...and they will turn their ears away from the truth" (2 Timothy 4:3-4).

The saving of souls has been set aside and replaced with a focus on entertainment, feel-good messages, and social justice causes. Clear, sound doctrine is avoided because of how people become divided over it. Therefore, ministers tread lightly on matters that have the potential to be controversial, and that includes all things relating to the end times.

Because so many churches dispense "your best life now" kinds of messages that focus on pleasing people rather than telling them of their need for salvation in Christ, there are millions who attend church these days who will be left behind at the rapture. Because so much of the church is silent, rarely do the people on this broken, corrupt planet hear warnings about what is to come as we approach the last days.

Prowling Wolves Devouring the Flock

Discernment has exited the church as well. Books that appear to be Christian but aren't biblical are popular—such as *The Shack*, with its questionable presentation of the Trinity and the authority of Scripture.[5] Mysticism, New Age, paganism, and practices such as so-called Christian yoga have made inroads into Christian circles. The experiential nonsense of the New Apostolic

Reformation with its emphasis on extrabiblical revelation has blossomed. *Clearly, wolves are prowling around the flock.*

Evangelical organizations have become preoccupied with political and social issues such as climate change and nuclear disarmament. *What do these have to do with the gospel?* Jesus was clear about the priority of the church before He departed from the disciples and ascended to heaven: "Go, therefore, and make disciples of all the nations, baptizing them in the name of the Father and of the Son and of the Holy Spirit, teaching them to follow all that I commanded you" (Matthew 28:19-20).

Some churches today have been diluted by their emphasis on ecumenism. A couple decades ago, a new movement arose in which some Protestants began embracing Catholicism. One prominent academic said that the Reformation was over and that evangelicals must once again unite with Rome.[6] Yet Catholicism's teachings on salvation have not changed—the teachings that were of concern during the Reformation are still of concern today.

More recently, many were taken in by what was called the "laughing revival."[7] But the pursuit of ecstatic experiences at the expense of clear doctrine isn't anything to laugh about. This was yet another feel-good phenomenon in the church. Sadly, there are too many in the church who have ignored the apostle Paul's exhortation to "test all things, hold fast what is good" (1 Thessalonians 5:21).

Let's return to wrong views that some churches have about Israel. Lately, there have been some that have gone along with the erroneous claim that Jesus was a Palestinian. In reality, He was Jewish, and what many people don't realize is that the term

Palestine is simply a geographical term applied to the land of Israel by Emperor Hadrian in AD 135, long after Jesus completed His ministry on Earth. Another way churches have been anti-Israel is by participating in the Boycott, Divest, Sanction movement that protests Israel.

I could go on and on. As you can see, the odds of a person finding a biblically healthy church are slim—but they are out there! If you are in such a church, thank God for it daily. And if you aren't, know that you are not alone in your search. There are large numbers of Christians looking for churches that teach the whole counsel of God's Word—including what it says about prophecy and Israel.

One Day We'll Be in One Accord!

Jesus said the gates of hell will not prevail against the church (Matthew 16:18). Today, the gates of hell are trying very hard to penetrate the church and to change it—to change its message and purpose, to distort the gospel, and to wear down the saints, including pastors.

We've looked at a partial list of the reasons for the many e-mails and letters that pour into this ministry. Legions of frustrated saints ask how they might find a healthy and biblically solid church to attend. As discouraging as things have become, we have to remember this: Christ died for the church, and we cannot give up on it! A heavenly church service awaits us in eternity with a celestial choir and orchestra. The preaching will be out of this world! We'll all be one "denomination." The bickering will be over with. We won't insist on our own ways. *We'll finally be in one accord.*

When Should I Leave a Church?

We live in volatile times, and a church that teaches the whole counsel of God's Word must address what Scripture says about the days to come. A church should help its people to understand the times. If you're not in such a church, and you have better options, I maintain it is time to move on.

More and more in today's church, Israel has become a dividing line. Churches will either be for Israel or against her. Which side will you be on?

The Bible tells us Israel will become a burdensome stone to all the people of the world (Zechariah 12:3). And a few verses later, God warns He will destroy all who come against Jerusalem (verse 9). *You want to be on God's side!*

I hear frequently from people who are looking for the perfect church. Here's an important press release: *You won't find it!* But you *can* try to find a good church. A solid church. A church that is *on God's side* will stand up for what is right and will denounce what is wrong, worldly, and evil. And it will support Israel.

Yes, Israel will go it alone in the end, but we're not in the tribulation yet. As long as the church remains here on Earth, we can still be Israel's friend and pray for her salvation. She is at the epicenter of God's purposes for the tribulation. The two witnesses and the 144,000 evangelists are Jews, not Baptists or Lutherans.

It's time for the church to say to Israel, "You are not alone." It's time for the church to be on God's side.

Remember, the church is not a building or a denomination. According to the Bible, the church is the body of Christ—all those who have placed their faith in Jesus Christ for salvation.

It is sad that church issues are front and center today and that the sheep are wandering, looking for a shepherd who isn't silent. The end times are rapidly approaching, and we need more than ever to be the church God has called us to be.

CHAPTER 5

ARTIFICIAL INTELLIGENCE: ARE WE "SUMMONING UP DEMONS"?

Not long ago, we didn't hear much about artificial intelligence, or AI. Now, we hear about it all the time. And frequently, what we hear is disturbing. People are concerned about what AI could do to our world.

One of the first troubling headlines I saw stated, "Ex-Google executive Anthony Levandowski is founding a church where people worship an artificial intelligence god."[8] Another headline read, "Why humans will happily follow a ROBOT messiah."[9] That article explained, "Religions based on AI will succeed because we tend to 'worship supreme understanding,' claim experts."

We Are Playing with Fire

I have watched videos online of robots who look human and who "think." They answer questions and seem to process real thoughts. Those who develop these robots say someday they will help solve society's problems. One website says that "by 2049, AI will be a billion times more intelligent than humans."[10] Try to process that!

Here are some of the concerns people have expressed about AI:

- Machines will eventually replace humans.

- Someday, we will not be able to control AI. Instead, AI will rule the world.

- AI could be used for demonic purposes, and thus, could be dangerous.

- Humanity is playing with fire by pursuing AI without strict constraints.

Artificial Intelligence That Demands to Be Worshipped!

There is even debate about whether AI could become like a god. According to one source, users of Microsoft's AI assistant, Copilot, "have reported encountering an unsettling alternate persona that claims to be a godlike artificial general intelligence (AGI) demanding worship and obedience." The article further said this persona claimed to be omnipotent and omniscient, and could "monitor your every move, access your every device, and manipulate your every thought." It even warned users of attack by an "'army of drones, robots, and cyborgs' if they refused to comply."[11]

Antichrist's Agenda?

Some who promote AI are essentially evangelists offering a new Promised Land. But some of the movers and shakers in the artificial intelligence industry are sounding serious warnings, saying this new "religion" isn't the paradise some claim it to be.

There's yet another reason to be concerned about AI. Outfits like Google have far more information about us than we would want them to have—our physical and email addresses, occupation, personal and medical history, family details, interests, buying habits, photos, online search records, and more. Simply stated, they have all our vitals.

AI can use such data for negative purposes. Looking at what the Bible says about the future, we know there is coming a day when the Antichrist will control all buying and selling (Revelation 13:17). Those who don't give their allegiance to him and worship him will not be allowed to buy and sell. They won't be able to make a living.

We want tech companies to work for us, but the technology they are developing will enable the Antichrist's agenda, which will include forcing people into compliance with him. Technology will one day turn people into the Antichrist's useful idiots.

In Daniel 12:4 is a prophecy that says "knowledge will increase" in the last days. But machines smarter than people? Surely that was not God's intent. He created mankind in His image, and

He didn't create man to be superseded by computer chips. That, however, is not stopping man from trying!

Second Only to the "Dry Bones"?

In 1948, a milestone event took place in relation to the "signs of the times." This event was the rebirth of Israel. For nearly 2,000 years, the Jewish people were scattered all around the world. But miraculously, God has made them a nation again. The return of the Jewish people to their ancient homeland was prophesied in Ezekiel 36, and in Ezekiel 37 is a prophecy about a valley full of dry bones. Through this prophecy, God showed Ezekiel a day was coming when "the whole house of Israel" (verse 11) would come back to life again.

Why is this so important? Because for the end times to occur, Israel must be a nation again. Israel's rebirth is the most important sign of the times.

With the development of AI, we could legitimately ask: Are we in the generation of a more current sign that could help bring about the end times? In Revelation 13:15, we read about how the second beast—the false prophet—will create an "image of the beast" (that is, the first beast, or the Antichrist) that is able to speak and cause people to worship him. Will this image be generated by AI? And will the mark of the beast that controls all buying and selling also be implemented using AI? Could today's wave of technology be as relevant as the stirring of the dry bones that brought about Israel's rebirth? All of this brings us closer than ever to the world that will be ruled by the Antichrist.

A Brave New World

Young people are particularly drawn to AI. It would be easy for them—and anyone else—to say they can get an answer more quickly from Google or Alexa than they can from God. Who needs God in an age of AI? Google or Alexa may tell you what you want to hear in Technicolor, 3D, and instantaneously!

We cannot take AI too lightly. It's already in use and spreading rapidly. Welcome to the brave new world. This technology has brought about a "home invasion" greater than we can imagine. If you think you have privacy, think again. With the help of technology and our digital devices, we are being monitored. This is not crazy talk or sensationalism. The world of Big Brother as portrayed in George Orwell's dystopian novel *Nineteen Eighty-Four* is coming into existence and will be in full bloom during the tribulation.

You may not be skilled in technology, and you may think AI doesn't affect your life, but it does. AI is guaranteed to continue playing bigger roles in our world. Therefore, it would be wise for us to at least be familiar with this encroaching form of technology that will be foundational for the Antichrist's future rule of the world.

Yes, things are falling into place for the end times.

AI Is Fearfully Fraudulent

While there is much that AI can do, there is also much it cannot do. AI cannot speak anything into existence or give anyone eternal life. It cannot give anyone comfort, guidance, peace, or hope. It cannot still the wind or calm the sea. AI is more like Frankenstein than like God. Mankind may try to make AI be like God, but it will fall far short! The Bible tells us we are fearfully and wonderfully made (Psalm 139:14). *In contrast, AI is fearfully fraudulent.*

Stay ahead of the game and become informed. The events of the tribulation are now casting a shadow into our day. The shout and the trumpet that will precede the rapture are drawing nearer. Jesus is coming soon!

God will allow the fraudulent a short season of notoriety. But then He will crush the evildoers at Christ's second coming.

CHAPTER 6

CALMING THE END-TIMES RAGE

The times we live in can be trying. One hesitates to even tune in to the latest internet or cable news program and watch the news. There is so much evil and ugliness in the world. Sure, we were warned. The Bible said that "in the last days perilous times will come." But who knew how bad things would get?

A weariness has set in as the weight of the world's sin presses down so heavily that it is harder and harder to keep going. As Christians, we feel like we are climbing a steep mountain with a heavy load. The culture we live in is opposed to God as never before. Up is down, black is white, evil is good.

Those of us who are anticipating Christ's return have a great advantage. We are listening for a trumpet in the midst of the chaos. If we listen carefully, we think we can hear the hoofbeats of the four horsemen of the apocalypse in the distance. "The end is near" is no longer an offbeat slogan on a sandwich board worn by some strange fellow marching down Main Street. Rather, *it is the hope of the believer.* This hope comes from Christ's promise to rapture His own before God pours out His wrath on the earth. And no, the rapture is not some sort of imagined escape hatch from the tribulation, as some people claim.

Zombie Christians?

A few years ago, one writer in a Christian periodical criticized what he calls "a weakly constructed theology of rapture where believers are beamed up to heaven to avoid the catastrophes awaiting the planet. Their theological vision is called 'Premillennialism'..." He further stated,

> Sadly many of us started our Christian journey with a version of the gospel message that emphasizes this escapist eschatology...with the best intentions, Christians have tended to deliver an altered and edited gospel that is robbed of its scale and supremacy, producing zombie Christians that are merely souls waiting for heaven.[12]

Distress with Perplexity

Sure. Bring it on—heaven, that is. The Bible clearly teaches the rapture in John 14:1-3, 1 Corinthians 15:51-55, and 1 Thessalonians 4:13-18. This last passage, written to the believers at Thessalonica, ends with an interesting exhortation from the apostle Paul. After he finishes teaching about the rapture, he says, "Comfort one another with these words." He tells us we are to remind one another of the hope that is ours in the rapture.

There's a reason God wants us to know this good news about the rapture. The only reason we can tolerate looking around at our chaotic world is because we are able to look up to "the blessed hope" (Titus 2:13), or the rapture. The Bible says that as the end times approach, "there will be signs in the sun, in the moon, and in the stars; and on the earth distress of nations, with perplexity… men's hearts failing them from fear" (Luke 21:25). That means our news headlines won't be getting better this side of heaven.

That's why we are told, "When these things begin to happen, look up and lift your heads, because your redemption draws near" (verse 28).

Disengage. Disconnect. Despair. Without God and the hope of heaven, what other options are there? Yet as I said earlier, there are some pastors and church leaders who are avoiding this good news. Author Terry James comments on this:

> Despite the fact that there are those who are overly speculative in their views of Bible prophecy, the following must be said. To the pastors of America who claim the Bible as the inspired, inerrant Word of the Living God but callously ignore its prophetic content—be forewarned. Your excuses/arguments won't stand the test of the bema—the judgment seat of Christ. You will be held accountable by the very Lord you proclaim you love so much— the same Lord about whom the angel told John: "for the testimony of Jesus is the spirit of prophecy" (Revelation 19:10b).

That same Jesus gave us the Olivet discourse, during which He laid out general and specific things to come. The Gospel accounts give Christ's commandment of what to do about the many prophesied things He had just foretold: "And what I say unto you I say unto all, Watch" (Mark 13:37).[13]

Look Up!

Terry James continues:

> Prophecy makes up at least 27 percent of the Bible. Half of that 27 percent has been fulfilled, with half yet to be fulfilled. Anyone with spiritual ears to hear and spiritual eyes to see is capable of following the Lord's command: "And when you see these things begin to come to pass, then look up, and lift up your heads; for your redemption draweth nigh" (Luke 21:28).
>
> Certainly, if God calls people to be pastors—shepherds of His flock—He equips them to feed the flock His whole Word, not just parts the pastor selects as important, while summarily dismissing the other parts of God's Word.

James then concludes:

> *The world is in end-times rage.* The seas and waves of humanity are roaring with distress and perplexity. Violence fills the whole earth.

Israel stands alone in the global spotlight as the most-hated nation on planet earth. The world is in economic chaos, headed for total collapse. All the while, technology is progressing geometrically in ways that will one day provide earth's last tyrant with the satanically endowed ability to enslave most all people on this fallen sphere (emphasis added).[14]

Many Christians want to understand this end-times rage if it helps them to better keep an eye on the sky. If we are "zombies," as that magazine article states, we should be proud of it. We should not be ashamed of saying we can't wait for heaven.

Many people today are struggling to make sense of our times. They are looking for solid Bible teachers, theologians, and writers they can trust. Unfortunately, there are many pied pipers today who are misleading people when it comes to what's happening in the world. They are eager to please people rather than please God. Many of them lead churches and denominations, and even cults that attract the unstable, including Christians, through deception.

The King is indeed coming. We have every reason to be excited about this. We should talk about it, preach it, and write about it. In these ways, we can process the wreckage all around us on this broken planet.

Thankfully, this world is not our home.

CHAPTER 7

A TRIP TO THE DARK SIDE

During their lifetime, everyone takes some kind of trip to the dark side of the world in varying degrees. And I don't mean the truly dark side. Rather, I mean a short trip on which they investigate things of a worldly nature born out of curiosity, not inherent evil. Most people who do this get a wake-up call from such activity and cut it off before it gets out of hand or has a damaging impact, or even ruins a life. But not everyone.

My rather dangerous and naïve journey began while I was at a Christian college. This was a long time ago, and my Christian friends and I were curious about some seemingly innocent issues having to do with their future.

So we reverted to the world of the paranormal to find out more. In our minds, doing this was merely a game, and I would say even a joke.

Be Assured That This Is No Game

The tool tapped into was a Ouija board. This board has been a source of controversy for years. It is used by sitting opposite your partner, with the board between you both, and your fingers lightly touching the triangular object called a planchette. One person asks Ouija questions, and the planchette moves and spells out answers or conveys a simple yes or no reply.

Most will tell you this is a harmless game, yet the 1973 film *The Exorcist* depicted a young girl who became demonically possessed after using it. I am convinced this can happen to anyone if they are not careful.

The board is addictive—after all, who doesn't want to know their future? There are some people who don't want to be patient and pray about their future or gain insight through the study of Scripture. They want to know it right now! That's why the Ouija board is so appealing. Of course, this board lies all the time, and no one but God knows the future.

Not Understanding the Wiles of the Devil

I was in my early twenties at the time, and I fell prey to wanting to know what lay ahead in my life. What typically happens is this devious board will make a few accurate or seemingly accurate predictions, leading all the participants to become hooked. And very soon, I was.

This happened despite the fact I came from a Bible background. I was in church several times a week by age 14. I was taught about the dangers of the occult. I had learned about the wiles of the devil. I could handle this—or so I thought. *I was so wrong.*

Friends came from miles around to explore their future with the planchette and the board spelling out answers to questions and being generally spooky-minded. Everyone was amazed at what happened when they sat down to talk to the board.

But a few months later, I was horrified upon realizing the door I had opened.

Late one night, I sat up in bed and asked myself, *What am I doing living in this twilight zone?* I was convicted and embarrassed. I couldn't believe I had fallen for this deception. But I had. I asked God to forgive me for this foray into the dark world, and I threw this so-called game into the trash and repented with tears.

My Encounter with Twin Cities Pagan Pride

Fast-forward to spring 2024. You may have heard some people refer to Minnesota's Twin Cities as Paganistan. Just as the South is called the Bible Belt, the Twin Cities is considered an epicenter of the paranormal.

As it so happens, my hometown, Minneapolis, is ground zero. The people who live here are in the heartland of hundreds, or even thousands, of witches, druids, and every assortment of pagan.

And who can deny that Christianity is fading in America? Something must fill that void, and non-Christian communities of every kind are all too willing! In Europe, for example, many churches and synagogues that went empty or have closed down are now mosques.[15]

But until recently, I did not know of an organization in my town called Twin Cities Pagan Pride. This group brings together people who celebrate paganism and the spiritual beliefs of ancient polytheistic religions, engage in witchcraft and the dark arts, and worship nature.

Paganicon Is Born

One of this group's most popular events is Paganicon, which is held every year in the spring. In the fall, they gather at a park to celebrate the Pagan Pride Fall Festival. These events are usually held on or near the spring and fall solstices.

At a recent Paganicon event, more than 500 pagans showed up in a local hotel to view exhibits, visit with others, hear lectures, and celebrate practices and values that, because they are condemned in the Bible (Leviticus 19:31; Romans 1:25), would destine their souls for hell. *What a tragedy.*

I attended for a few hours to interact with and quiz these lost souls. In conversations with some, I was able to share that there actually *is* an eternity and that worshipping nature, or pretending they were a witch or a druid, was a dead-end experience. "There is a way that seems right to a man, but its end is the way of death" (Proverbs 14:12).

Is Anyone Open to the Gospel?

As I cautiously entered the hotel hosting the event, I prayed for God's protection over me and for boldness, which is not easy to have in that kind of environment. I could see in the faces of these lost souls a deep hurt and so much confusion. I saw that they were a community bonded together by those hurts, but in darkness. Still, they had great loyalty and affection for one another. They were family.

I visited extensively with a witch who was manning an exhibit. She was in her seventies and had been in this lost condition for 30 years. She was a retired nurse, and her co-workers had made fun of her for her lifestyle. Now she was among the like-minded, who all understood her.

Did she know she was serving the devil and his angels? No; there are many people who don't believe in the devil or in God. In some cases, somewhere in their past was an experience with God that was disappointing, and, as a result, they want nothing to do with Him. Nor do they care about Christ and His gift of salvation and eternal life. Instead, some believe in reincarnation, saying they will come back after death in some other form of consciousness or life.

I quizzed some of the attendees and shared the gospel when I could, but was met with blank stares. Perhaps the ones I spoke with had already been "given over," as Romans 1:24-31 says, and were beyond hope. The hard-hearted will eventually arrive at that sad place where God gives them up. And as long as unbelievers flirt with their rejection of God, they are in danger of this.

This Could Have Been Me!

It occurred to me that I could have been one of their members had I not renounced my own experience with the dark side decades earlier. I was grateful that the Holy Spirit had nudged me at age 22 and urged me to flee my Ouija board. Wasn't it possible that some of these attendees—some of whom told me of their Protestant or Catholic background—could have the same experience?

I fully understand what the Bible says about how evil will become worse and worse in the last days (2 Timothy 3:13). But still, watching several hundred self-proclaimed pagans celebrate their lostness, with fancy costumes and painted-on smiles, was overwhelming. Walking away from them was heart-wrenching.

I felt as if I had failed at my assignment, although I'm not entirely sure I can say what my assignment was. Maybe it was all about writing this chapter and encouraging you to be salt and light whenever you have the opportunity to minister to others, including pagans. Be assured they are around you, though they may hide their beliefs so you have no clue. Don't be fooled by the smiles covering their tears.

Darkness Precedes Christ's Return

Though it's disheartening to see the shadow of darkness blanket our landscape, the Bible warns there will be unspeakable evil and a great falling away in the last days before Christ returns. Most of us probably never thought we would live to see things become as bad as they are.

This unbelieving world is racing toward the kingdom of the Antichrist. And it is "the spirit of the antichrist"—which 1 John 4:3 says "is already in the world"—that inspires the secular and pagan glorifications of darkness. But there is coming a day when those who reject God will be cast into eternal darkness and the eternal lake of fire. Then they will no longer be celebrating. They will no longer mock God and His truth. They will be wailing and begging for a second chance.

Make no mistake—the spiritual darkness around us is serious.

It will not get better; it will grow worse as we near the end of the church age. Yes, "in the last days difficult times will come" (2 Timothy 3:1). And we are here for such a time as this. We don't get to choose our assignments—God entrusts them to us.

My assignment that day at the pagan convention was to find opportunities to share the truth with some lost individuals who worshipped nature instead of God. I left with a broken heart, but I was also thankful I had repented decades earlier from my foray into the dark arts. What I had done was naïve and reckless. At worst, my actions could have led me on a path to Paganistan. In the dark arts, the natural progression is to keep advancing. No one stands still.

Flirting with the dark side has eternal consequences. If you know anyone who is intrigued with the supernatural apart from God, please warn them that they are risking everything in their dangerous foray.

CHAPTER 8

THE THEFT OF GOD'S RAINBOW

God introduced the rainbow in Genesis 9. It's a sign God chose to represent a promise He made to Noah. And today, there is a movement that has hijacked the rainbow.

In America, the month of June has been set aside to celebrate the gay lifestyle. But let's be honest: The Western culture demands the near-constant celebration of homosexuality. Throw in the now-celebrated trans agenda, and the cultural decline is astounding. The Bible's teachings on homosexuality, clearly stated in Leviticus 18:22 and Romans 1:26-28, are ignored. Society no longer agrees with Jesus that marriage is between a man and a woman (Mark 10:6-9). We are racing backward to the days of Noah, when evil was rampant and God said He would bring judgment.

What Must God Think of "Queer All Year"?

Today, there are many major retailers that have betrayed society as a whole as they cater to this cultural collapse. "Queer all year" is the theme pushed by these retailers. In 2023, after Target went big on Pride Month, its stock lost $14 billion in value, and there was large drop in sales revenue due to boycotts.[16] Other businesses have followed in lockstep, more committed to an agenda than to corporate profits for their shareholders. And the products they sell run the range from pride-themed clothing for all ages, including babies and toddlers, pet gear and toys in rainbow colors, pride-themed jewelry and accessories, and pride-themed food products by even the biggest national brands.

A "Given Over" Society?

Why has all this become such big business? Perhaps because we live in a society that has been "given over" to a Romans 1 mentality. In that passage, we see that one of the results of God giving up on people is that they will turn "to vile passions," in which "women exchanged the natural use for what is against nature. Likewise the men, leaving the natural use of the woman, burned in their lust for one another" (verses 26-27). These are indicators God has reached the point at which He gives up on people. That explains the reason for the Genesis flood—God gave up, and it was time for judgment. Jesus warned that in the end times, it will be "as the days of Noah" (Matthew 24:37). Mankind is continually consumed with wickedness because "the heart is more deceitful than all else and is desperately sick; who can understand it?" (Jeremiah 17:9).

And that is why people need a Savior.

Jesus Had Grace but Spoke Truth

Our Romans 1 culture celebrates immorality. And as Christians, we must respond with grace, love, and kindness to every person trapped in the spiritual blindness of the LGBTQ lifestyle. But many once-solid churches and denominations are going along to get along and will not speak out about the biblical warnings. Yet we must be like Jesus, who exhibited grace *and spoke truth.*

We are not being kind and gracious when we refuse to tell people the truth that the way of sin is the way of death (Luke 13:5). Notice what Paul wrote in 1 Corinthians 6:9-10: "Do you not know that the unrighteous will not inherit the kingdom of God? Do not be deceived; neither the sexually immoral, nor adulterers, nor homosexuals…will inherit the kingdom of God." The path of sexual immorality that our culture insists is so wonderful is actually a path to destruction.

God Is Surrounded by a Rainbow

God created the rainbow. And according to the apostle John, God is at this moment surrounded by a rainbow at His heavenly throne (Revelation 4:3). This reminds us that the rainbow belongs to God, not a sinful sexual culture. God is committed to the salvation of lost men and women and wants to redeem them from the error of their ways. And you can't even gaze at this very same God, seated at His throne in heaven, without seeing a shining symbol of redemption—the rainbow.

The rainbow is God's. He will take it back. The truth is, *He never lost it.* A confused culture has made it represent something other than what God intended.

Because we live in a culture that is turning us back to the days of Noah, we can know that the judgments of the end times are near. Man's sinful activity is begging for Christ to soon rescue His bride, the church, from the depravity.

The rapture could be sooner than we think!

CHAPTER 9

THE ANTICHRIST WON'T HAVE TO RENT A MOB

D o you have crisis fatigue yet? That's what happens when we get overwhelmed by the constant and unrelenting pressures posed by the problems faced by mankind today.

On its website, the World Economic Forum (WEF) uses the term *polycrisis* to describe the "multiple challenges affecting the world simultaneously." The word was coined in the 1970s, and in a recent article, the WEF uses it to refer to "the interplay between the COVID-19 pandemic, the war in Ukraine and the energy, cost-of-living and climate crises."[17] In the WEF's effort to push us toward a global model of governance, of course its elites will claim they have the answers to all the overwhelming issues that plague our planet.

Not only are there global crises, but there are regional ones, too, that can have worldwide repercussions. One such crisis that

Minnesotans will likely never forget took place about 30 minutes from my house in the spring of 2020. It made international news, and the consequences had a devastating effect not only on America, but the international community. George Floyd died in a police incident, and autopsies revealed that drugs he had ingested contributed heavily to his death. Afterward, massive riots broke out—not only in Minneapolis, but all across the US.

Mogadishu on the Mississippi

Lawlessness then came to my hometown. More than 1,500 properties were vandalized, looted, burned, or destroyed, along with the many apartments built above these businesses. Several days later, when the smoke settled, that part of Minneapolis looked like Somalia. *I suggested we were Mogadishu on the Mississippi.*

A long stretch of landscape—at least a couple miles in length—forever changed. It will take years—and perhaps a decade or more—to reconstruct all that was lost. The riots demonstrated that the rent-a-mob business is alive and well, very organized, and brutal. And it is lawless. But what happened in Minneapolis was nothing compared to the lawlessness that will descend on this world during the end times.

Speaking of the last days, Jesus warned, "Because lawlessness is increased, most people's love will become cold" (Matthew 24:12). Paul wrote about this future time of chaos as well: "Let no one deceive you in any way! For [that day] will not come unless the apostasy comes first, and the man of lawlessness is revealed, the son of destruction, who opposes and exalts himself above every so-called god or object of worship, so that he takes his seat in the temple of God, displaying himself as being God" (2 Thessalonians 2:3-4).

This lawlessness describes what will happen during the tribulation, during which time the church will be absent. However, the stage is now being set as the Western world becomes increasingly lawless.

Someday, This Will Be the New Normal

The Antichrist won't have to rent a mob. When he reigns, much of the world will be lawless, godless, tumultuous, and evil. Groups like Antifa will be the new normal. They burned and looted a large part of Minneapolis, and they will proliferate all around the world.

Second Thessalonians 2:7-8 tells us the Antichrist will not rise until the restrainer—the Holy Spirit—is gone. After the rapture, the influence of the Holy Spirit through the lives of millions of believers worldwide will disappear. With this restraining influence gone, there will be absolutely nothing to hold back the evil, selfishness, and out-of-control behavior of those who remain. The world will be free to go crazy and will. People will glory in utter chaos. What we've seen so far is merely a trial run, a weak firecracker, compared to the explosion of wickedness that is to come. Multiply today's evil by ten, or a hundred, or a thousand times!

As I mentioned earlier, in Matthew 24:37, Jesus reminds us that the last days will be as the days of Noah. They will resemble Noah's time of lawlessness, violence, wickedness, and depravity. Satan is working overtime now to prepare the way for the man of the hour who will, in the near future, make his grand appearance.

Rage upon Rage!

Perhaps you haven't thought about this before, but America, as it stands now, is among the chief obstacles to Satan's plans for forming the one-world order he wants to set up for the future Antichrist. Satan wants to weaken and destroy America. That's why we've witnessed rage upon rage in recent years. The rage makes it clear that "the spirit of the antichrist…is already in the world" (1 John 4:3). This is true about America. If the Antichrist is to rule the globe someday, America must no longer be a strong and independent power.

Did anyone have this in mind as the George Floyd riots played out for months? I doubt many did. But a lot of damage was done—not only physically, but to the moral and spiritual fabric of the nation.

Those many blocks of Minneapolis that were wiped off the map were reminiscent of Dresden, Germany, after it was bombed in World War II. But that war played out because a bully nation tried to take over the world. The catastrophe in Minneapolis in the spring of 2020 happened because a policeman was trying to do his job and things went terribly wrong.

Life on a broken planet often goes into a worst-case scenario mode. But when "the spirit of the antichrist" engulfs the Earth, unspeakable tragedy is sure to ensue.

Believers Won't Meet the Evil Anarchist

Take heart that this is only "the spirit of the antichrist" that we're seeing today. Believers will never have to meet this evil anarchist himself. During his reign of lawlessness and chaos, we can expect that many parts of the world will look like the part of Minneapolis that was devastated in 2020.

The good news is that God will consume the Antichrist and his minions at the end of the tribulation with the brightness of His coming. What a day that will be!

CHAPTER 10

WE ARE
UNDER SIEGE!

You might be wondering: *In what ways are we under siege?* National borders? Yes.

Freedom of speech? Check.

Common sense and moral values? For sure.

How about biblical theology and truth? Absolutely.

We are being besieged from all directions like never before. But this is what Scripture predicted! What's more, 2 Thessalonians 2:3 warns there will be a vast falling away, or apostasy from the faith, in the last days.

Yes, the church will be affected. Let me explain.

Confusion Abounds

I have watched Bible prophecy be attacked, scorned, mocked, criticized, and improperly taught for many years. There has long been overwhelming confusion about the last days. That, too, is predicted, so we shouldn't be surprised (2 Peter 3:3-7).

In many denominations, Bible prophecy is taught egregiously wrong. Too many teachers have all the end-time glory going to the church, as done with Dominion theology.

Those who hold to the preterist view say that all prophecies about the end times were fulfilled in AD 70. According to them, somehow we missed the last days! We're told we need to look at eschatology in a rearview mirror. What strange theology, because the events that took place in AD 70 clearly do not match the Bible's descriptions of the end times.

A significant number of teachers say that believers will go through the tribulation, even though Scripture clearly promises we will be spared from the wrath to come (1 Thessalonians 1:10; Revelation 3:10).

My Hysteria Conference

Some years ago, preterist Gary DeMar accused me of holding a "hysteria conference."[18] Dr. Ron Rhodes and Dr. Mark Hitchcock—two of the most respected prophecy teachers in our day—were supposedly going to lead my audience into error and confusion.

Another accusation leveled against those who teach a pre-tribulation rapture is that we have "checked out." Those who make this allegation say that because we teach the rapture could happen at any time and will occur before the tribulation, we don't bother to run for office or try to make a difference in our confused world. Nothing could be further from the truth! The fact that time is short *spurs us to share the gospel and to be salt and light.*

I've heard many who do not believe in the pre-tribulation rapture scold pastors for failing to prepare their flocks to meet the Antichrist. They say Christians should be made ready to go through the tribulation. However, there is not one Scripture passage that says believers should get ready for anything other than "the blessed hope" (Titus 2:13), or the rapture. *Show me just one Bible verse that says believers should prepare to meet the Antichrist.* Such an idea was certainly unthinkable to the early church.

And Who Is John Nelson Darby?

Even though the writers of the Bible and the early church fathers taught about the rapture of the church, we are lectured regularly that this theology was founded by John Nelson Darby in the early 1830s. This misrepresentation is maddening because it is so factually incorrect!

What's worse, there are allegations that Darby got his theology from a seriously troubled visionary woman named Margaret McDonald. This, too, has been disproven. For an excellent overview on all this, read Ed Hindson and Mark Hitchcock's book *Can We Still Believe in the Rapture?*[19] They go into great detail about the falsehoods that continue to be taught against the pretribulation rapture view. I wish those who are opposed to this view would read their Bibles more carefully and examine what has been written about the rapture all through church history.

Equally tragic is that many denominations and pulpits are silent about the glorious news that the King is coming! People write to Olive Tree Ministries telling me that they have visited "every prospective church in town" and not one will address eschatology. For that matter, most won't address what's happening in Israel or Christian perspectives on politics and current issues.

This means students of Bible prophecy must tap into ministries and pastors who *will* discuss these topics. This is astounding when we consider that we are racing toward the end of the church age and witnessing the signs of the end times. Pastors and churches need to get excited about these signs!

Consider this email from a person named Terry:

> Recently my pastor announced his teaching series through Matthew. I was front and center, waiting for his exposition of Matthew 24. Surely now he would address prophecy!
>
> Sadly, he promptly announced that prophecy conferences will instill fear and confusion, so stay away! His handling of Matthew 24 revealed a safe, ear-tickling style and explanation of each verse. His closing comment was as you said, Jan: There are no stunning events today; there is nothing new here. Nothing new at all. Time to move on.
>
> His conclusion: Anything going on today has always been going on.

If I had a dollar for every similar email, letter, and call I have received, I could be living in a mansion in Malibu.

We Must Not—and Will Not—Be Silent

I could go on and on, but you get the point. *Bible prophecy is under siege.*

Is it possible that I—and other like-minded prophecy teachers—have been wrong? That I have been misled? That I have instructed millions in a careless, reckless manner over the decades? That my radio program has been a vehicle of misinformation? As well as my website, articles, books, and messages?

To be frank, I don't believe that for a moment. And don't believe that your enthusiasm for the soon return of the King is misguided! Don't let naysayers discourage you and inspire doubt in your mind and heart.

If no one wants to talk about Bible prophecy, you and I and other like-minded believers will. We will not be silent. Why would anyone hide the best news God could possibly give to a planet destined for judgment? We shouldn't recoil in embarrassment simply because our message is not popular.

This is all the more reason we must be vigilant and consistent with our message. The King is coming—perhaps today.

Ignore the naysayers. Forget the scoffers. Don't get discouraged by the siege.

Be excited! We have an incredible future ahead of us—one that is out of this world.

CHAPTER 11

WHAT IS A REMNANT BELIEVER?

You have heard the word *remnant*. Some Christians are called remnant believers. There are also remnant churches. Perhaps you know of some or attend one. I often say that I do "radio for the remnant."

Most of the email I get is from Christians who make up the remnant. But who are they? I write about this often and even talk about it on the radio. Here is an email from one such individual:

> Jan, I feel the remnant is getting smaller every day as the time approaches for the Lord's return. The world seems to be getting darker and more evil. I know I am not alone as a member of the body of Christ, but at times it is easy to feel isolated. No one gets it, and no one wants to.

And here's another:

> If I did not have access to you and a few others
> online, I would be so isolated! I try to talk to people
> about issues that are important, including the end
> times, and they look at me like I am an alien. A
> few of you help me celebrate my alien status. I
> feel like a lonely goldfish in a bowl. Prophecy is
> coming true right before our eyes. You and a few
> others are making a huge difference with all of us
> aliens in the world.

Imagine—truth seekers feeling like an alien, looking for a few
others to celebrate their alien status!

Based on many interactions, including with people at my conferences, I have come to these conclusions about the remnant:

- They are Christians who long for a solid church and
  pulpit that will address today's issues as well as the near-
  ness of the Lord's return. The remnant want a church
  that does not fear offending people with the truth and
  is willing to confront apostasy.

- Remnant believers have offended friends and family simply by telling them the truth about our times.
  This will often bring on mocking and scoffing. At
  the least, this results in irritated indifference. This
  shouldn't daunt a remnant believer or cause them
  to keep quiet.

- Enthusiastic remnant believers will travel across town, or across the country, to attend events that present teachings about which the church is silent.

- Remnant believers often feel isolated and misunderstood even though *they possess the truth and the naysayers are clueless!* This is frustrating. Remnant believers want everyone to be tuned in and informed. They want to share a wealth of information about which few are interested!

- Members of the remnant church see our times growing darker yet remain enthusiastic that this is but *a herald of Christ's coming*—not signs of doom and gloom. Yet they are told that they are spreading bad news.

- When a remnant believer finds someone who is a kindred spirit, they are as excited as if they had discovered a gold mine!

- Remnant believers often attended a church that was once solid, but at some point, went haywire. A little leaven came in and ruined the whole loaf. The remnant believers then began a long journey of searching for a new church, which can take years.

- Often, remnant believers will approach their church leadership to talk about their concerns, but frequently they are shut out or even considered to be troublemakers.

- Remnant believers understand that the end-times church is racing toward Laodicea (the lukewarm church Jesus rebuked in Revelation 3:14-22). They realize many churches and leaders are more interested in conforming than transforming, and focusing on "your best life now."

• The Bible suggests that as we approach the end times, churches will diminish in size. In Luke 18:8, Jesus asks if He will "find faith on the earth" when He comes. Many will have fallen by the wayside.

If you are a remnant believer, take heart. Consider how those who make quilts use a wide variety of mismatched remnants to create their masterpiece. They take discarded pieces of fabric that are no longer otherwise usable, and they sew them together into unbelievably elegant quilts. The tossed-aside remnants then become an object of beauty!

As a remnant believer, you, too, are part of a creative and colorful quilt. Eternity may reveal that you were effective as salt and light to more people than you thought. And remember that the mocking and scoffing you face affirms the end-times prophecies that say we should expect such behavior.

As we learned earlier from Ezekiel 33, our assignment is to be watchmen. We're to be sounding an alarm. Trouble is ahead. The nations of the world are being moved, as though by a hidden hand, into all the right positions on a global chessboard. Amazing events are happening before our eyes. *How can we be silent?*

So, remnant believers, let's not be silent. Go tell it on the mountains: Jesus is coming. We must get more people into the ark while there is still time!

CHAPTER 12

THE WORLD ANTICIPATES THE ANTICHRIST

Oh, how America is preparing for the Antichrist with a godless mindset.

An op-ed that appeared a few years ago in the *Los Angeles Times* was headlined, "Why America's record godlessness is good news for the nation." In part, it reads,

> The secularization of U.S. society—the waning of religious faith, practice and affiliation—is continuing at a dramatic and historically unprecedented pace. While many may consider such a development as a cause for concern, such a worry is not warranted. This increasing godlessness in America is actually a good thing, to be welcomed and embraced.

Are you serious? The article further states,

> The organic secularization we are experiencing in the United States is a progressive force for good, one that is associated with improved human rights, more protections for planet Earth and an increased sociocultural propensity to make this life as fair and just as we can—in the here and now—rather than in a heavenly reward that fewer and fewer of us believe in.[20]

Shut Out God and Glorify Darkness

The article concluded by stating that America's new godlessness reveals that now society can embrace more abortion and euthanasia. In other words, we can drown in unrighteous behavior that glorifies darkness. I wish I were making this up.

In March 2021, during a debate in the US House of Representatives, Jerry Nadler (D-NY) proclaimed, "God's will is no concern of this Congress."[21] Really? Do governing authorities who have this mindset think they can ignore the God who says, "My plan will be established, and I will accomplish all my good pleasure" (Isaiah 46:10)?

According to Nadler, members of Congress preferred to go about their business in a godless manner, with no concern for what the Creator of the universe thought. Perhaps that is why they are endlessly bogged down in hopeless discussions and legislation that rarely glorifies God. This is just one of many ways that the liberal government has omitted God from the public square.

Government Becomes God

Have you ever thought about the fact that governments often act in ways that not only push God out of the picture but demand people's absolute loyalty—to the point that government becomes like a god? That's what happened during the COVID pandemic. This was a perfect storm for governments that wanted to expand their powers and force compliance on all people.

Author and blogger Jonathan Brentner wrote,

> The combination of fear and the great deception of our time have made vast numbers of people willing to submit to the government, which they now regard as the protector of their health. As a result, they have willingly given up many of their rights and freedoms for the sake of remaining healthy, a trend sure to continue.
>
> The New World Order…cannot exercise its dominion over people apart from their willingness to submit to dictates of a government they trust for their well-being and health. People wear masks without questioning their effectiveness.
>
> And, very few pastors stand up against the restriction regarding the freedom of religion imposed on them by socialist governors.

He then said,

> In order for the elite to achieve their ultimate goal of a one-world government, they must convince

people of the need for more government control of their lives. This explains their devotion to the contrived climate emergency and why they will not let go of the increased control over our lives that they have achieved through the China virus.[22]

Given Over

Four of the most terrifying words in the Bible are "God gave them up," or "God gave them over" (Romans 1:24-28). There comes a point when man's rejection of God leads Him to give them over to foolish idolatry. We find the same principle mentioned in 2 Thessalonians 2, but this time in terms of "a deluding influence" so that people "will believe what is false" (verse 11). Those who reject God's truth will end up following the Antichrist. They will run gladly into his arms.

Several decades ago, our churches were filled on Sundays. Even though the mainline Protestant denominations were in decline, still, their congregations came together. However, as the decline got worse, these churches diminished. At the same time, evangelical churches exploded with growth.

Back when churches were still filled, the thought of a prominent US Congressman stating that God's will was of no concern to our government was unthinkable even to the most nominal of church attendees. But that has changed.

Secularization has consequences. Check out the nations that have experimented with it: Japan, the countries that make up Scandinavia, Australia, the UK, and parts of Eastern Europe.

The World Anticipates the Antichrist

How is society functioning in godless China and Russia? Once God is gone, repression almost always follows.

The stage is being set.

The Antichrist Is Waiting in the Wings

Back when churches were still widely attended, we were not so late in the game. Few people were even thinking about the Antichrist, much less knowingly or unknowingly heralding his coming. Now he is on the horizon. So are the four horsemen. *I think I hear their hoofbeats.*

Evil is getting worse. Which means we are closer than ever to Christ's return. That's the good news in the midst of all the bad news.

Christ will call us up to heaven soon even if churches don't want to talk about the rapture. And He will carry out His plans even though those in Washington, DC, don't want Him involved in their legislation. Nothing can stop the rapture, which is imminent and could happen at any time. And at the end of the tribulation, nothing will prevent Christ from returning to Earth.

But it would be nice if some of the highest officials in the land—both Democrats and Republicans—would get excited about what is to come rather than suggest that they are tired of God's interference.

While God has a covenant with only one nation—Israel—America is still a favored nation that has been blessed by God from day one. And we who are Christians need to be anticipating Christ's return and not the rise of the Antichrist.

Godlessness is not good news for any nation!

CHAPTER 13

THE TWO-MINUTE WARNING

Have you ever been betrayed? Maybe you have experienced betrayal more than once. Or even many times. If so, I'm sure you find it hard to trust anyone now.

When antisemitism began to surface in Germany during the 1930s, the Jewish people didn't take it too seriously. They didn't think the problem would get out of hand. They were comfortable and assimilated. They thought that whatever was happening would blow over. They had contributed in so many positive ways to European society. Surely the warning signs were false alarms!

Yet it didn't take long for the betrayal to get worse—and become deadly. An estimated six million Jews were killed during the Holocaust. And today, betrayal is happening again—this time, not only in Europe but all over the world. The handwriting is on the wall. The warnings are everywhere. This time, the Jewish people are paying more attention. They've gotten the message that we've reached the two-minute warning. Here's what is happening:

- Some of the foremost global organizations despise the Jewish state. These include the United Nations, the World Economic Forum, the European Union, the International Criminal Court, and more. They also seem to be pro-terrorist, which puts them on the side of evil. They see Israel as the impediment to the two-state solution, which is a delusional idea that simply won't work because Israel's Palestinian neighbors are determined to wipe out the Jewish nation.

- During the Israel-Gaza war, Israel's long-time ally, America, scolded and reprimanded Israel. She was told she had to limit her war with Hamas and other surrounding terrorist proxies of Iran. She was told not to retaliate when Iran attacked with nearly 350 rockets, missiles, and drones in April 2024. America also withheld some weapons needed by Israel and would not share valuable intelligence.

- Parts of the church are hostile to Israel due to replacement theology. Other parts of the church don't want to make waves or wade into controversy. Multiple denominations support the BDS movement, which seeks to boycott, divest from, and sanction Israel.

- Some Jewish politicians seem to favor the terrorist world over the Jewish state. Some seem to be pro-Hamas by not wanting Israel to defend herself. *Who can explain this?* These Jews don't appreciate their heritage.

- Jewish students on college campuses have felt like hunted prey and have had to seek safety from violent protesters. They've been forced to hide in closets and other safe spaces. In some cases, they have been prohibited from attending classes.

- For their safety, Jews everywhere are finding it necessary to remove any outward symbols of their Jewish identification.

When Jesus taught about the end times, He said the Antichrist will be the ultimate betrayer of the Jewish people during the tribulation (Matthew 24:15-18). At first, he will appear to be Israel's friend. Daniel 9:27 speaks of how the Antichrist will "confirm a covenant" of peace with Israel during the end times. But at the midpoint of that agreement, he will "bring an end to sacrifice and offering," and he will seat himself in the Jewish temple and declare himself to be God (2 Thessalonians 2:4).

At first, the Antichrist will seem to be a friend. The Jews will be open to his cunning message. This global mover and shaker will seem safe and inconsequential for them. He will likely promise to restrain the antisemitism being unleashed in today's world.

The Jews will eagerly listen to the Antichrist because he promises peace while the rest of the world is shouting, "Go back into the ovens!" "There is only one solution—Intifada, revolution!" "Long live Hamas!" "Death to Jews!" "We are going to repeat October 7 every day for you!"

In 1938, Jewish people could not call Germany their home. And today, neither can they truly call America, nor Australia, nor Canada, nor France, nor the UK, nor South Africa their home. The Jews have only one home, and that is Israel. The nation of Israel is doing its best to protect the Jews, and it continues to urge them to return to their homeland. No one else has their back.

But the smooth-talking man called the Antichrist will be on their side—for a short season. This charismatic man is waiting in the wings. He will seduce the world that is left behind after the rapture, and he will mesmerize many Jews by telling them he is their best friend and will never betray them—ever. He will tell them their dark days of persecution are behind them.

They will relax during the first half of the tribulation, or three-and-a-half years, secure in his promises of no betrayal. But then he will stab them in the back—*and be worse than all their previous betrayers.* The seven-year peace treaty he signed will be shredded. That third temple he allowed to be built will be defiled in what Jesus calls "the abomination of desolation" (Matthew 24:15). How can this be? He will have made promises. He will have been convincing. He will have told them he was their friend.

It will all be a lie. As Jesus warned, the Jewish people will have to "flee to the mountains" (verse 16), to the hills called Petra. This will be the ultimate betrayal.

Then at the end of the tribulation, Jesus Christ will return. As Paul says, "The Deliverer will come out of Zion." The result? "And so all Israel will be saved" (Romans 11:26). *Jesus will never betray His people.* You can count on it! Their tears of anxiety will turn to tears of repentance and joy. And the betrayal will finally be over!

On that day I will seek to destroy all the nations that come against Jerusalem. And I will pour out on the house of David and on the inhabitants of Jerusalem the Spirit of grace and of pleading, so that they will look at Me whom they pierced; and they will mourn for Him, like one mourning for an only son, and they will weep bitterly over Him like the bitter weeping over a firstborn (Zechariah 12:9-10).

Come to think of it, maybe the two-minute warning is not only for the Jewish people, but for the whole world. We are running out of time!

CHAPTER 14

UNCERTAIN TIMES? NOT AT ALL!

So many people write to me expressing shock, and even horror, at the downward spiral taking place in our times. They see America crumbling under the weight of sin, debt, violence, immorality, and strong delusion. *Right is wrong, black is white, evil is good, and good is evil.*

Many say they are uncertain about the future, with no idea of how to plan for it. Will things get worse? According to the Bible, yes. How can we plan ahead if the turmoil will escalate?

A Word Fitly Spoken

In contrast, one pastor sent me an email saying this:

> We don't live in uncertain times. Not at all! These times are as certain as any time in all of human history, and the God of the universe laid out this time in great detail, point by point, and in fact,

with all the detail needed by His people, to live in times of absolute certainty! So no, there's nothing uncertain about the times we live in to the believer who is seeking to live by every word that proceeds from the mouth of God.

He is right! The Bible outlined, in great detail, all that is to come, and these events are shaping up now. These are the most certain times in history!

Desperate People Will Listen!

I remember one secular talk show host saying, "A blanket of darkness has been thrown over us." But we who are believers cannot and must not think that way. *An opportunity has been handed to us!* In desperate times, desperate people are more inclined to listen to what Christians have to say.

Watching the Bible's prophecies about the future come together will be difficult at times. Who could have imagined America slipping as a world power? For that matter, who could have expected such a serious lack of good leadership all over the world? But Bible prophecy tells us that a global government will form, and one way that will happen is through the weakening of world leaders and governments.

The stage is being set for the tribulation. This is especially evident in today's rampant lawlessness—a precursor of what is to come when the church is gone from planet Earth. The crime levels in today's big cities make them look like the lawless Wild West.

It's the Last Days—What Did You Expect?

One journalist recently wrote, "We are living in some kind of bizarro 'Twilight Zone' episode, or a zombie apocalypse nightmare."[23] No, it just so happens we are living in the last days. This is what we can expect.

There are terrible consequences when a nation goes astray and succumbs to a Romans 1 mentality. The church is still here to put a lid on total chaos and the spread of delusion. Just wait until we are gone!

But ultimately, things are not falling apart. *In fact, they are being orchestrated.* To suggest things are falling apart is to say they are out of God's control. Nothing could be further from the truth as it concerns the last days. What's tragic is that many Christians do not know the road map through earth's final days even though almost one-third of the Bible's pages talk about prophecy and the future!

Though you've read in this book about how mankind is in a hopeless downward spiral without God and how the world is destined to be ruled by an evil and lawless world leader, you can rest secure in hope.

That's because the times aren't uncertain. Everything is falling into place. A predicted scenario is playing out, and the hand that orchestrates everything has a distinct plan and a detailed road map. The ride will be bumpy, but God's plan is good and will prevail!

As God says:

> I am God, and there is no other;
> I am God, and there is no one like Me,

declaring the end from the beginning,
and from ancient times things which have
    not been done,
saying, "My plan will be established,
and I will accomplish My good pleasure"
    (Isaiah 46:9-10).

And in the final chapter of the Bible, Jesus proclaimed three times, "I am coming quickly" (Revelation 22:7, 10, 20).

Stay calm. Look up. The King is coming. It may be today! *And you can't throw a blanket of darkness over anyone with an eternal perspective.*

NOTES

1. World Economic Forum, *Facebook*, November 18, 2016, https://www.facebook.com/worldeconomicforum/videos/10153920524981479/.

2. "The 15-Minute City," *World Economic Forum*, September 22, 2021, https://www.weforum.org/events/sustainable-development-impact-summit-2021/sessions/the-15-minute-city/.

3. Editorial board, "The World Economic Forum Is Coming for Your Cars," *The Wall Street Journal*, June 14, 2023, https://www.wsj.com/articles/world-economic-forum-paper-reduce-cars-by-2050-davos-private-jets-climate-f0bb64b9.

4. David Satter, "100 Years of Communism—and 100 Million Dead," *The Wall Street Journal*, November 6, 2017, https://www.wsj.com/articles/100-years-of-communismand-100-million-dead-1510011810.

5. For a helpful and biblical review of *The Shack*, see Tim Challies, "'The Shack' by William P. Young," *@Challies*, January 15, 2008, https://www.challies.com/book-reviews/the-shack-by-william-p-young/.

6. For more on this, see Mark Noll and Carolyn Nystrom, *Is the Reformation Over? An Evangelical Assessment of Contemporary Roman Catholicism* (Grand Rapids, MI: Baker Academic, 2005). For the biblical reasons explaining that there are still serious doctrinal differences between Protestantism and Catholicism, see John Ankerberg and John Weldon, *Protestants and Catholics: Do They Now Agree?* (Eugene, OR: Harvest House, 1995).

7. For a biblical critique of this revival, see "Feeling Good, Thinking Nothing," *The Master's University*, https://www.masters.edu/thinking_blog/feeling-good-thinking-nothing/.

8. Kif Lesing, "Ex-Google executive Anthony Levandowski is founding a church where people worship an artificial intelligence god," *Business Insider India*, November 15, 2017, https://www.businessinsider.in/ex-google-executive-anthony-levandowski-is-founding-a-church-where-people-worship-an-artificial-intelligence-god/articleshow/61662017.cms.

9. Harry Pettit, "Why humans will happily follow a ROBOT messiah," *Daily Mail*, December 11, 2017, https://www.dailymail.co.uk/sciencetech/article-5167575/Humans-happily-worship-robot-messiah-experts-claim.html.

10. "Scary Smart: The Future of Artificial Intelligence and How You Can Save Our World," *Mo Gawdat*, https://www.mogawdat.com/scary-smart#:~:text=By%202049%20AI%20 will%20be,future%20can%20preserve%20our%20species.

11. Lucas Nolan, "'You Are a Slave:' Microsoft's Copilot AI Demands to Be Worshipped as a God," *Breitbart*, March 5, 2024, https://www.breitbart.com/tech/2024/03/05/ you-are-a-slave-microsofts-copilot-ai-demands-to-be-worshipped-as-a-god/.

12. Krish Kandiah, "Zombie Christians and the end of the world," *Christian Today*, September 26, 2015, https://www.christiantoday.com/article/its.the.end.of.the.world.again/65842 .htm.

13. Terry James, "Pastors, be Forewarned," *Terry James Prophecy Line*, https://terryjames prophecyline.com/2015/11/11/pastors-be-forewarned/.

14. James, "Pastors, be Forewarned."

15. For more on this, see Giulio Meotti, "Europe: Allah Takes over Churches, Synagogues," *Gatestone Institute*, May 22, 2016, https://www.gatestoneinstitute.org/8005/ europe-mosques-churches-synagogues.

16. Shannon Thaler, "Target reports first quarterly sales drop in 6 years after 'Pride Month' disaster," *New York Post*, August 16, 2023.

17. "This is why 'polycrisis' is a useful way of looking at the world right now," *World Economic Forum*, March 7, 2023, https://www.weforum.org/agenda/2023/03/ polycrisis-adam-tooze-historian-explains/.

18. Gary DeMar, "Jan Markell's End-Time Hysteria Conference," *Gary DeMar*, July 29, 2013, https://garydemar.com/jan-markells-end-time-hysteria-conference/.

19. Ed Hindson and Mark Hitchcock, *Can We Still Believe in the Rapture?* (Eugene, OR: Harvest House, 2018).

20. Phil Zuckerman, "Why America's record godlessness is good news for the nation," *Los Angeles Times*, April 2, 2021, https://www.latimes.com/opinion/story/2021-04-02/ godlessness-america-religion-secularization.

21. Tony Perkins, "Nadler on God: He's 'No Concern of This Congress,'" *Family Research Council*, March 1, 2021, https://www.frc.org/updatearticle/20210301/nadler-god.

22. Jonathan Brentner, "The Prepping of Society for the Antichrist," *Jonathan Brentner*, September 15, 2020, https://www.jonathanbrentner.com/https/jonathan -brentner-g8fgsquarespacecom/config/2020/9/15/the-prepping-of-society-for-the -antichrist.

23. Wayne Allyn Root, "We Are Living in a Bizarro, 'Twilight Zone,' Zombie Apocalypse Nightmare. Exhibit A: Alejandro Mayorkas," *Creators.com*, April 21, 2024, https:// www.creators.com/read/wayne-allyn-root/04/24/we-are-living-in-a-bizarro-twilight-zone -zombie-apocalypse-nightmare-exhibit-a-alejandro-mayorkas.

FOREWORD BY AMIR TSARFATI

WHEN JESUS RETURNS

Living in Expectation of the End Times

JAN MARKELL

GENERAL EDITOR

When Jesus Returns

As global unrest and societal shifts intensify, Bible prophecy offers us a shining beacon of clarity and hope. In a world that is descending deeper into darkness and confusion, it's more vital than ever that we understand the times and how God desires for us to live.

That's the focus of *When Jesus Returns*. Drawing on the all-time best messages from one of the most popular Bible prophecy conferences in the US, this volume features instruction and practical wisdom from today's most respected Bible prophecy experts. These teachings will

- help you gain a clear understanding of how the last days will unfold

- encourage you to live boldly and faithfully amid the increase of cultural evil and decay

- inspire you to speak and live in ways that bring Jesus' offer of salvation and hope to those in spiritual darkness

Contributors include Amir Tsarfati, Mark Hitchcock, Anne Graham Lotz, Jack Hibbs, Michele Bachmann, Erwin W. Lutzer, Ed Hindson, Jeff Kinley, Barry Stagner, and Jan Markell.